P9-CEB-354

# RE-CYCLES

MICHAEL ELSOHN ROSS

ILLUSTRATED BY GUSTAV MOORE

THE MILLBROOK PRESS
BROOKFIELD, CONNECTICUT

In memory of my pal Wendy P. — M.R.

To Rebecca — G.M.

Library of Congress Cataloging-in-Publication Data
Ross, Michael Elsohn, 1952-
Re-cycles / Michael Elsohn Ross ; illustrated by Gustav Moore.
p. cm. — (Cycles)
Summary: Describes the cycle of soil decomposition and the water cycle, as well as how to develop a compost pile for recycling peapods and other garden products into compost to feed a garden.
ISBN 0-7613-1818-6 (lib. bdg.)
1. Soil formation—Juvenile literature. 2. Hydrologic cycle—Juvenile literature. 3. Compost—Juvenile literature. 4. Life cycles (Biology)—Juvenile literature. [1. Soils. 2. Hydrologic cycle. 3. Compost. 4. Life cycles (Biology) 5. Cycles.] I. Title: Recycles. II. Moore, Gustav, ill. III. Title.
S592.2 .R66 2002    551.3'05—dc21    2001044772

Published by The Millbrook Press, Inc.
2 Old New Milford Road
Brookfield, Connecticut 06804
www.millbrookpress.com

Everything on Earth is always changing. Sometimes these changes repeat over and over in patterns called cycles.

# SOIL CIRCLE

A little seedling sprouts in the shade of bigger trees.

Its tiny roots reach down into the ground for nutrients and water, which help it to grow.

At first the seedling is no taller than a turtle . . .

. . . but each year it grows higher and higher, until one day, a hundred years later, it is a grand old tree.

Children swing from its limbs, birds build nests on its branches,
and caterpillars dine on its delicious leaves.
Every autumn the tree drops acorns, which are eaten by the jays,
squirrels, and deer.

After many, many more years, the tree becomes old and weak. Beetles lay their eggs under the bark, and the young grubs munch on the living tree.

Woodpeckers peck into the tree to find and eat the grubs. They make nest holes in the rotting trunk to raise their babies in safety.

The old tree becomes weaker still, and soon mushrooms sprout from its trunk. The mushrooms are part of a fungus that eats the trunk and digests the mighty roots.

One day, during a wild and furious storm, the old tree sways in the wind and then crashes to the ground.

Before long a city of tiny creatures appears inside the skeleton-like remains of the tree. Termites, beetles, and sawflies make tunnels as they feast on the wood.

Slowly, over many years, the bugs and fungi take apart the tree. It becomes a mound of rotten wood that adds a new richness to the soil. The nutrients from the old tree can now help other trees grow.

One day a tree seedling sprouts on the old tree's grave.
Its tiny roots reach into the ground for water and nutrients,
and soon it grows tall from the rich soil, water, and sunshine.
One day it will be a grand old tree that will then die and add
a new richness to the soil.
One day it will complete the soil circle.

## DECOMPOSITION FACTS

- Moisture and warm temperatures make a tree decay faster.

- Soil is made up of a combination of minerals, dead plants, and dead animals.

- Millions of insects can live in a dead tree.

# WATER CYCLE

Out of the sky falls a little drop of water.

It lands on a leaf and drips to the ground.

It joins other drops, and together they trickle into a stream.

Gurgling and splashing, they glide over pebbles and rocks. Like a silver snake, the stream slides to the sea. The drop is now one tiny part of the big salty ocean.

Each day water drops evaporate and disappear into the air as they change to water vapor.

One day the sun's rays heat up the drop until it also changes to vapor.

The little drop floats up into fluffy clouds, where it joins more droplets.

When the droplets of vapor become chilled by cold air, they begin falling as raindrops.

This time the water drop falls into a dirty puddle on a school playground. That very afternoon the heat of the sun changes the drop to vapor, and once again it floats up into the sky to join a cloud.

Later it falls again as snow high in the mountains and doesn't flow back to the ocean until the next spring.

Year after year the drop cycles from earth to air, from dirty water to clean vapor.

Every day, water drops ride the never-ending water cycle.

## WATER FACTS

- Most of the water on Earth is found in the oceans and is salty.

- The average-size tree can release a hundred quarts (ninety-five liters) of water a day through its leaves.

- Most of the water on Earth has been around for billions of years.

# HUNGRY COMPOST PILE

Nature recycles water and soil. You can recycle too. You can take used cans, paper, and plastic to a recycling center, where they can be processed to make new products for people to use—and recycle once more! You can even recycle some of your kitchen and yard waste.

Max and Julia have a big pile in their backyard where they put
banana peels, apple cores, eggshells, bread crusts, leftover rice,
old leaves, grass clippings, and other stuff that will turn into soil.  It is
called a compost pile.

The compost is alive with worms, rolypolies, and other little creatures.
Millions of bacteria, which are tiny creatures too small to see, live in the
compost and quietly dine on the leftovers from the kitchen and garden.

Max and Julia add dry leaves to keep the compost pile from getting smelly.
They add water to keep it from getting too dry.

As the critters munch the stuff in the pile, they create a rich fertilizer called compost. It is like the rich humus from the forest floor.

Week after week Max and Julia feed the pile, and within a couple of months they have compost to feed their garden.

The compost helps the cucumbers, peas, and watermelons to grow big and healthy.

After Julia and Max eat the cucumbers, peas, and watermelons,
they feed the peels, pods, and rinds to the compost pile.
Gardens feed composts and composts feed gardens.
That's another cycle!

## COMPOST TIPS

- Don't put meat or bones in compost; they will attract animals.

- Keep the compost moist, but not soggy.

- Start a compost pile by mixing kitchen wastes, dry leaves, and a little garden soil.

# ABOUT THE AUTHOR AND ARTIST

Michael Elsohn Ross lives at the entrance of Yosemite National Park, California, on a bluff overlooking the wild Merced River. Both his wife and teenage son are published poets and avid outdoors people. For over twenty-five years Michael has been teaching Yosemite visitors about the plants, animals, and geology of the park. He leads classes and backpack trips for the Yosemite Association and is the educational director of Yosemite Guides. His work in the park and as a science educator have inspired him to write over thirty books for young people, including **Become a Bird and Fly** and **Earth Cycles**, **Life Cycles**, and **Body Cycles**, the other three volumes in the Cycles series.

Growing up in rural Maine, Gustav Moore's boyhood adventures in the woods and fields of his family's farm have given him a deep appreciation and love of the natural world. His colorful and detailed watercolor paintings reflect this beauty and wonder of nature. In addition to the three earlier volumes in this series, he has illustrated **Stonewall Secrets**, which was recognized as a 1998 Notable Children's Book by Smithsonian, and **Everybody's Somebody's Lunch**. Gustav Moore works and lives in Maine, where he still wanders the open pastures of the family farm, finding inspiration in the cycles of nature.